Learning Together

Counting

Designed and illustrated by
Andy Everitt-Stewart

© Peter Haddock Limited, Bridlington, England.

See how the numbers 1 – 20 in the squares are written – from the red dot to the blue dot – and trace over the dotted lines. Then try by yourself.

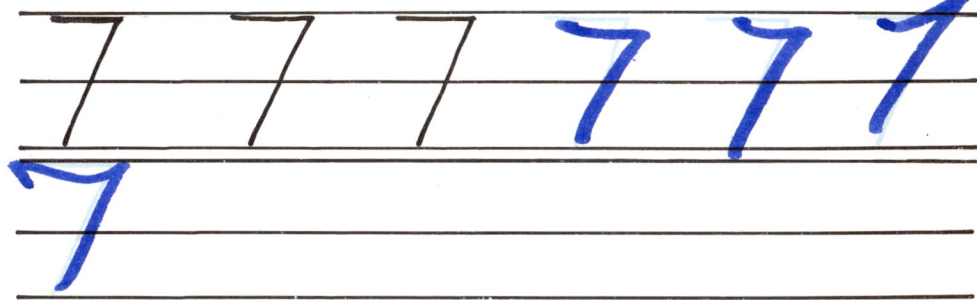

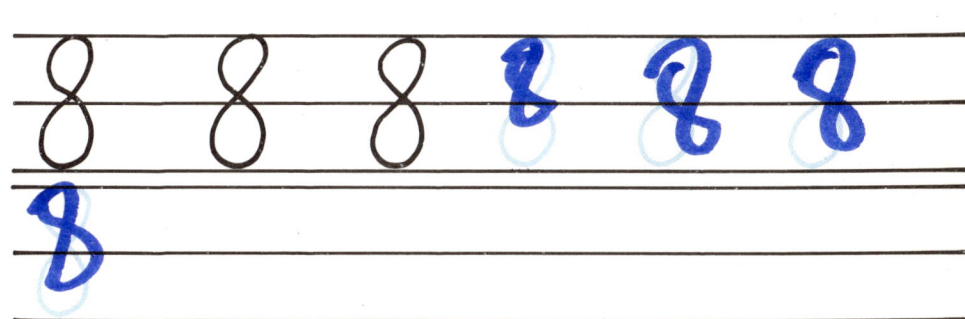

6	6 6 6 6 6 6	
	6	
7	7 7 7 7 7 7	
	7	
8	8 8 8 8 8 8	
	8	
9	9 9 9 9 9 9	
	9	
10	10 10 10 10 10	
	10	

| 11 | 11 | 11 | 11 | 11 |
11

| 12 | 12 | 12 | 12 | 12 |
12

| 13 | 13 | 13 | 13 | 13 |
13

| 14 | 14 | 14 | 14 | 14 |
14

| 15 | 15 | 15 | 15 | 15 |
15

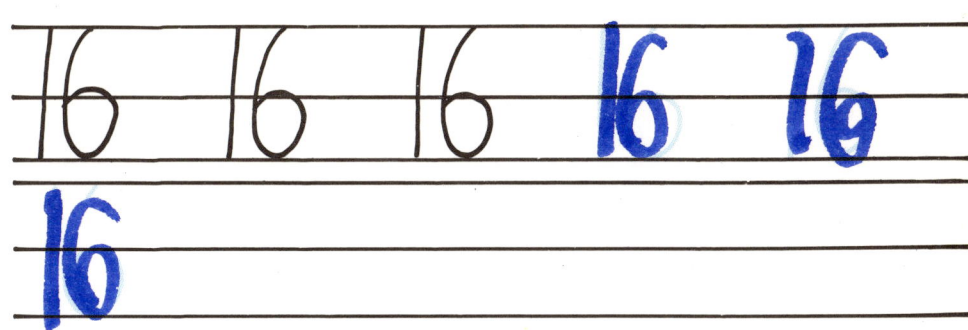

16	16 16 16 16 16
	16
17	17 17 17 17 17
	17
18	18 18 18 18 18
	18
19	19 19 19 19 19
	19
20	20 20 20 20
	20

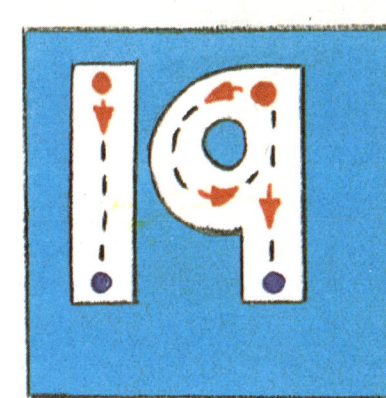

Trace over the blue numbers in the lines and then write the same numbers all by yourself.

1 1 1 1 1 1

2 2 2 2 2 2 2 2 2 2
2

3 3 3 3 3 3 3 3 3 3
3

4 4 4 4 4 4 4 4 4 4
4

5 5 5 5 5 5 5 5 5 5
5

6 6 6 6 6 6 6 6 6 6
6

7 7 7 7 7 7 7 7 7 7
7

8 8 8 8 8 8 8 8 8 8
8

9 9 9 9 9 9 9 9 9 9
9

10 10 10 10 10 10 10 10 10 10
10

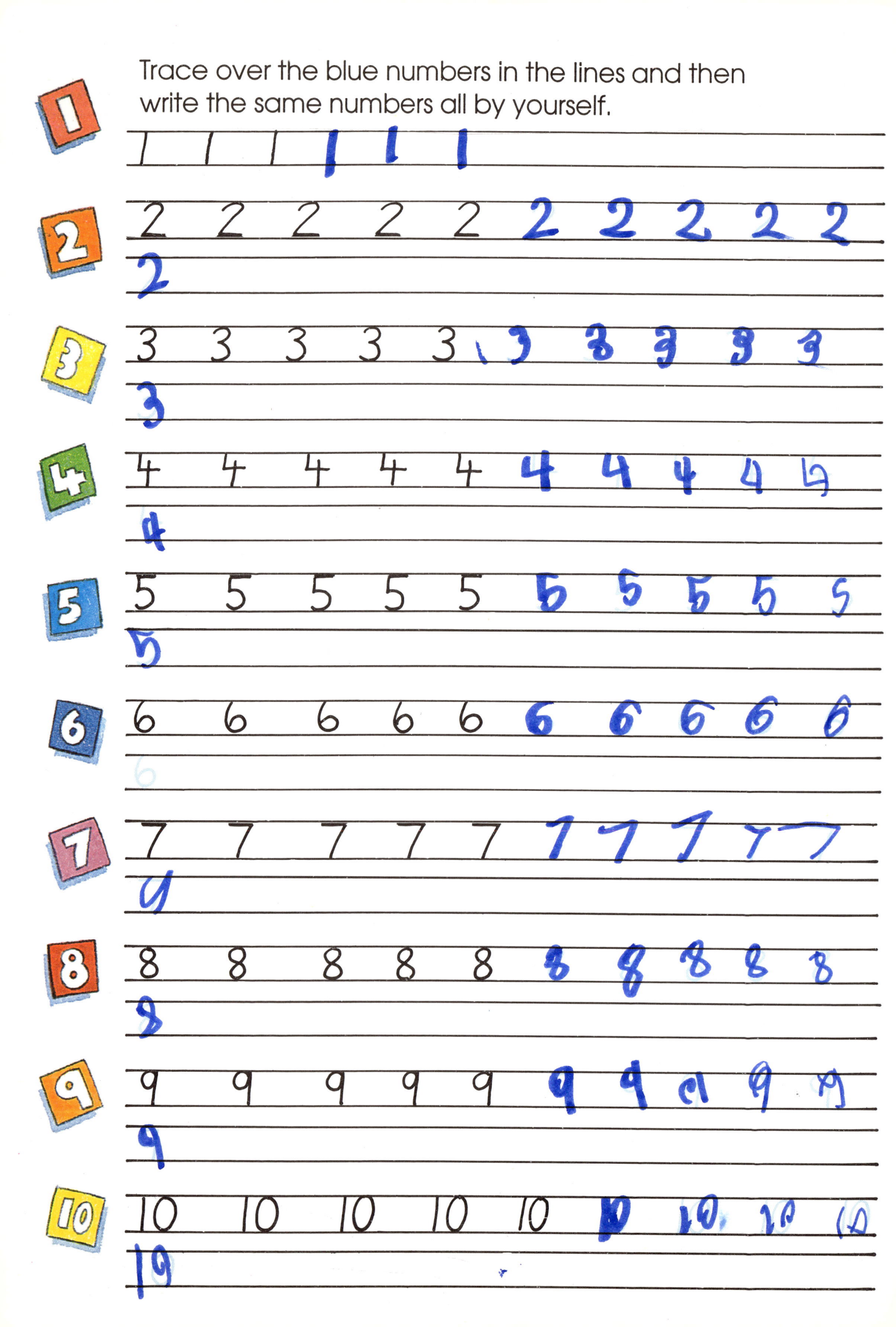

11
11 11 11 11 11 11 11 11 11
11

12
12 12 12 12 12 12 12 12 12
12

13
13 13 13 13 13 13 13 13 13
13

14
14 14 14 14 14 14 14 14 14
14

15
15 15 15 15 15 15 15 15 15
15

16
16 16 16 16 16 16 16 16 16
16

17
17 17 17 17 17 17 17 17 17
17

18
18 18 18 18 18 18 18 18 18
18

19
19 19 19 19 19 19 19 19 19
19

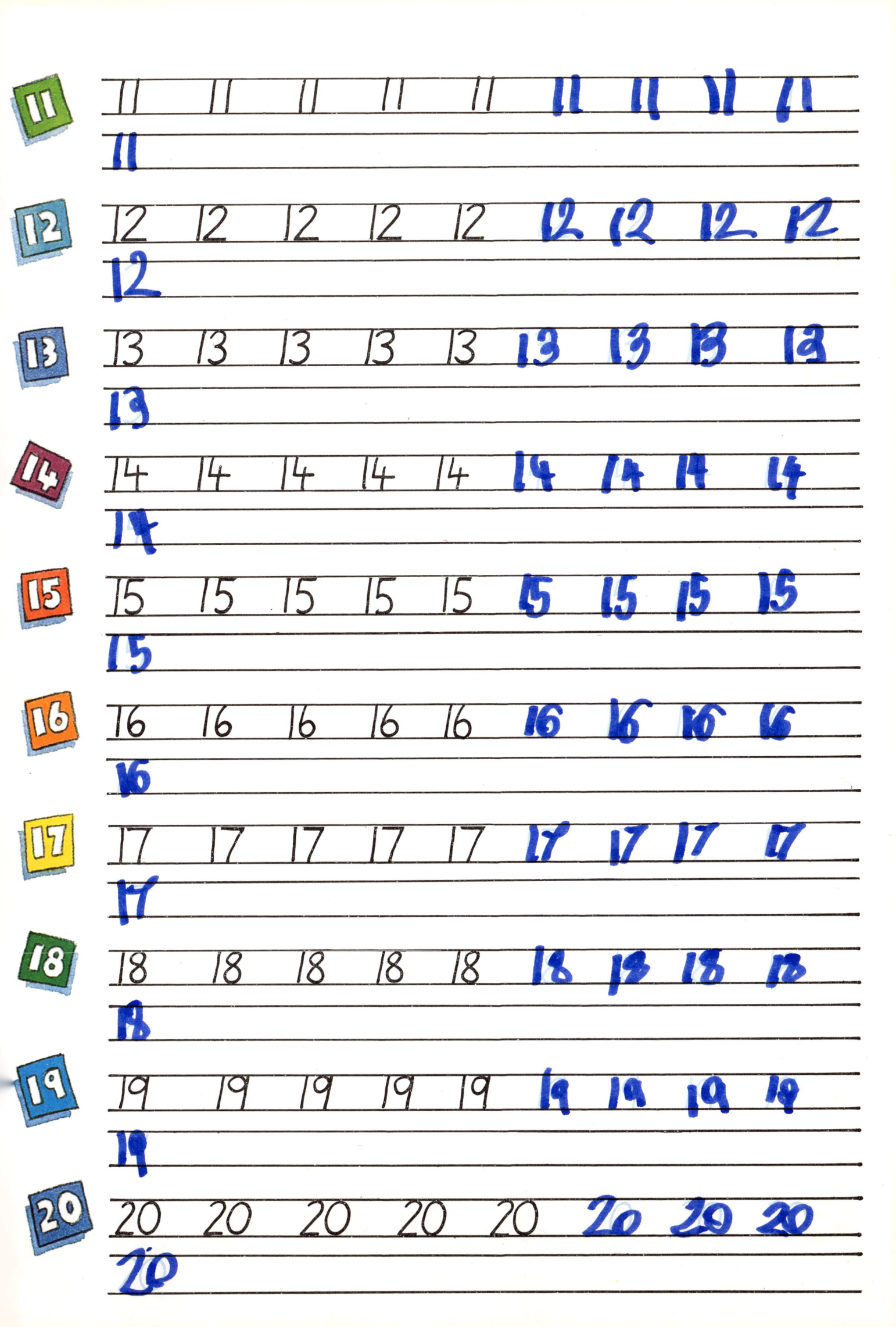

20
20 20 20 20 20 20 20 20
20

one

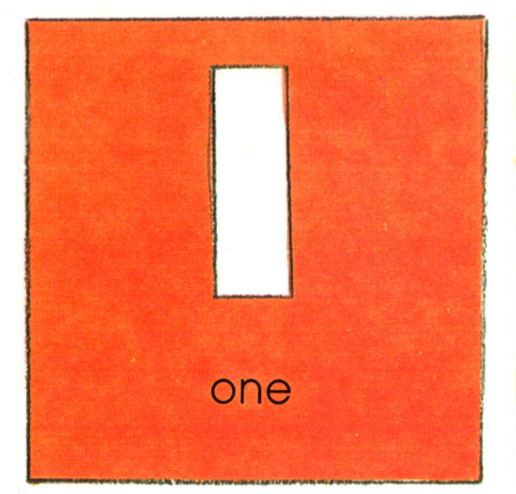

Draw the figure 1 by following the dotted lines and then colour the picture.

2
two

2 2 2 2 2 2 2

Look at these fruit. Draw a ring round the only 2 that are the same.

3 three

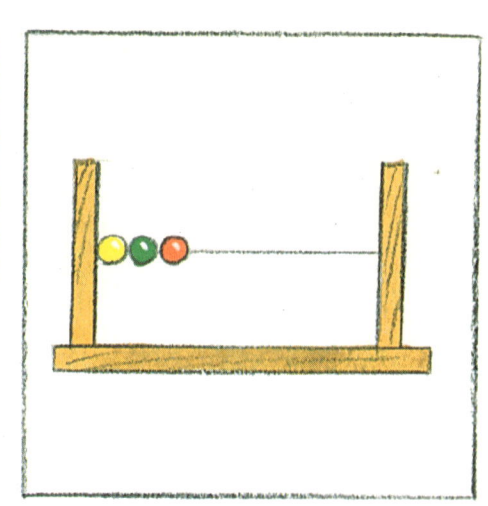

3 3 3 3 3 3 3 3

Which pile of presents has only three packages? When you have found the right pile write the figure **3** on its label.

4

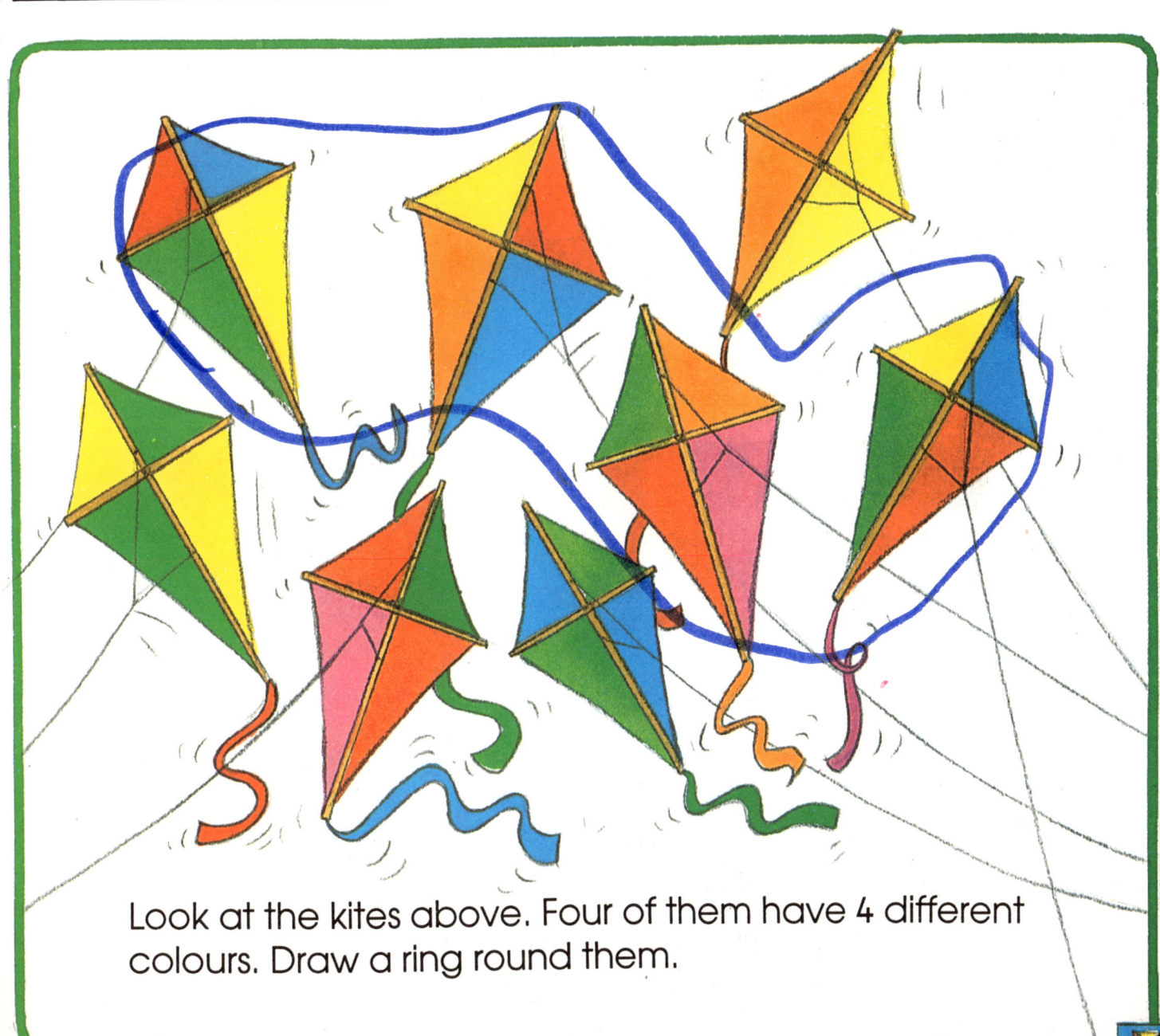

four

4   4   4   4

Look at the kites above. Four of them have 4 different colours. Draw a ring round them.

5
five

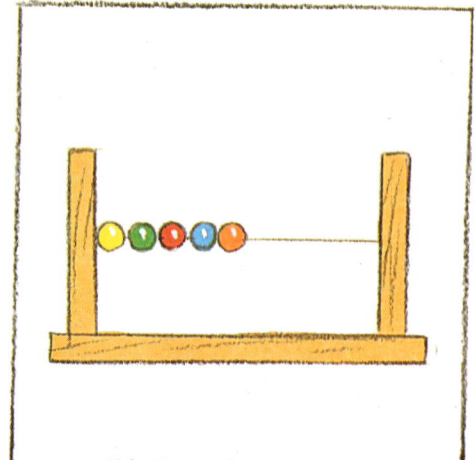

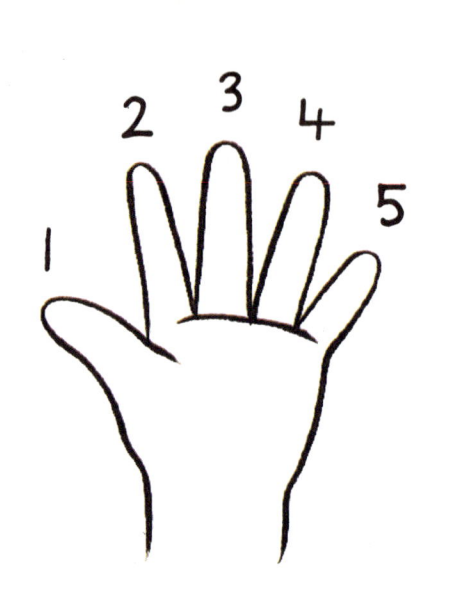

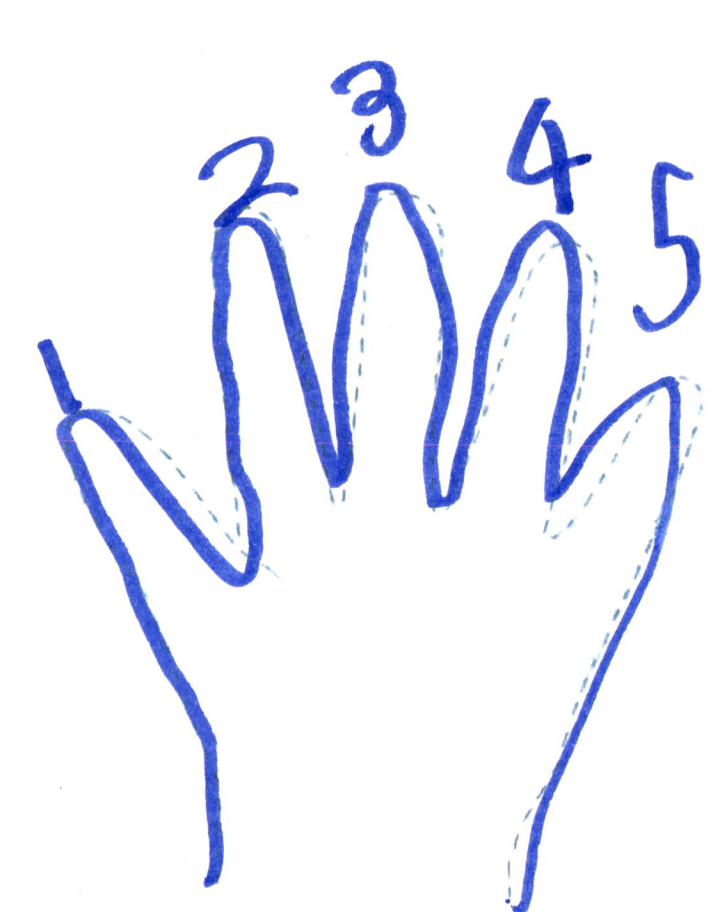

5 5 5 5

Count the number of fingers and thumbs on each of your hands. Draw in the hand above by following the dotted lines and write in the number of fingers and thumbs.

6 six

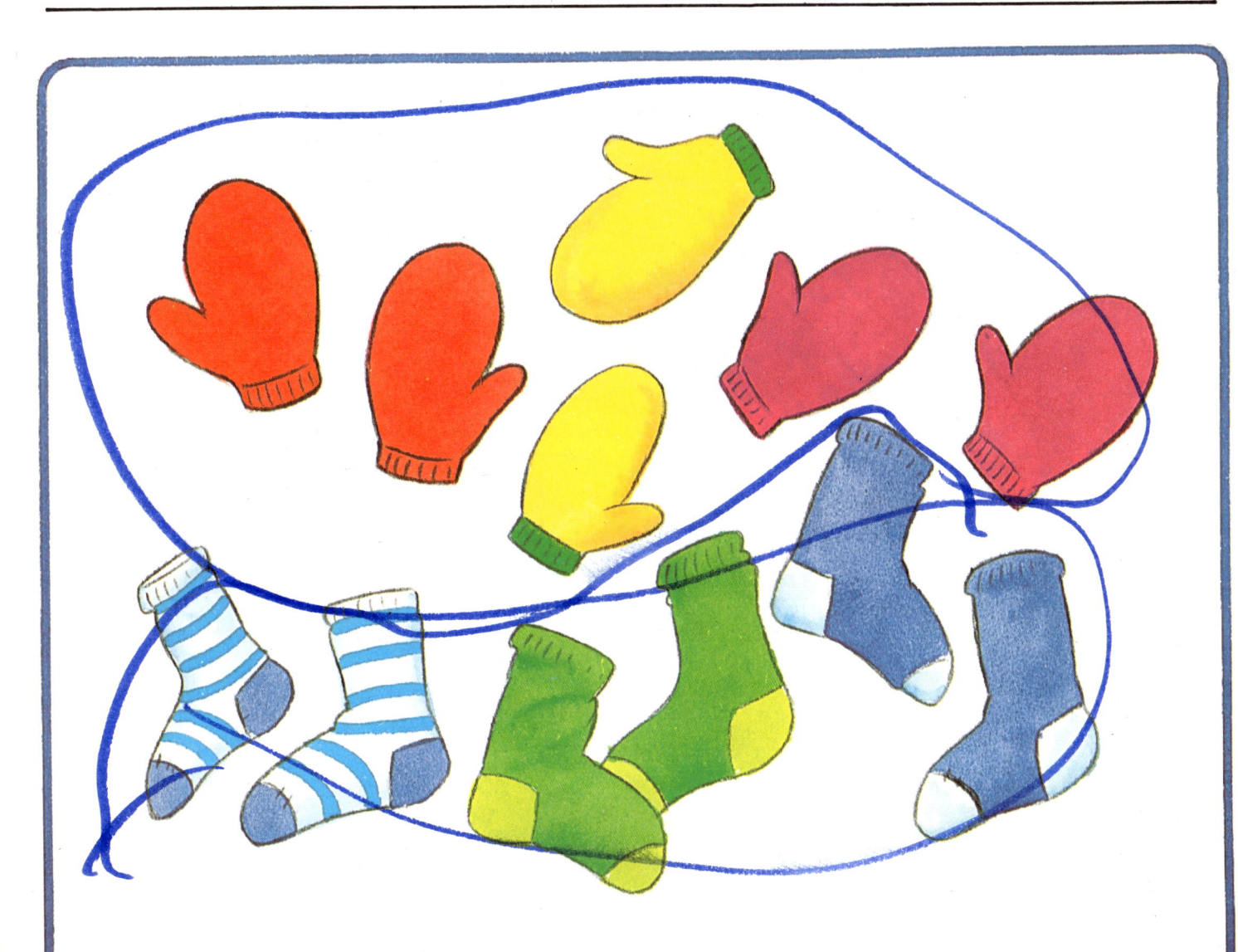

6 6 6 6 6 6 6 6

Divide the objects above into two groups of 6 and draw a circle round each group.

7
seven

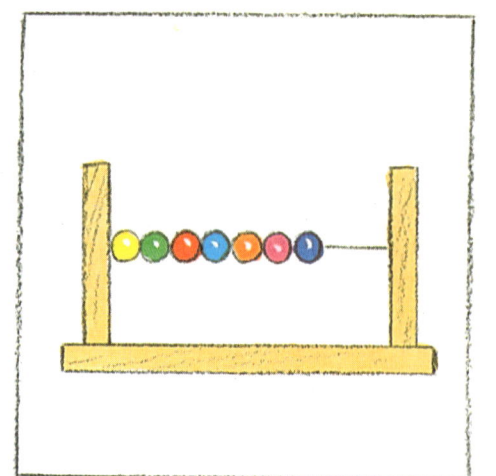

A rainbow always has 7 colours. Look at the numbers on the crayons and colour the rainbow by matching the numbers.

8

eight

8 8 8 8 8 8 8 8

Count the number of tentacles on the octopus and then draw them in by following the dotted lines.

nine

q q q q

Only one of these flags has **9** stars. Count the number of stars on each flag to see which one it is and draw a circle round it.

10 ten

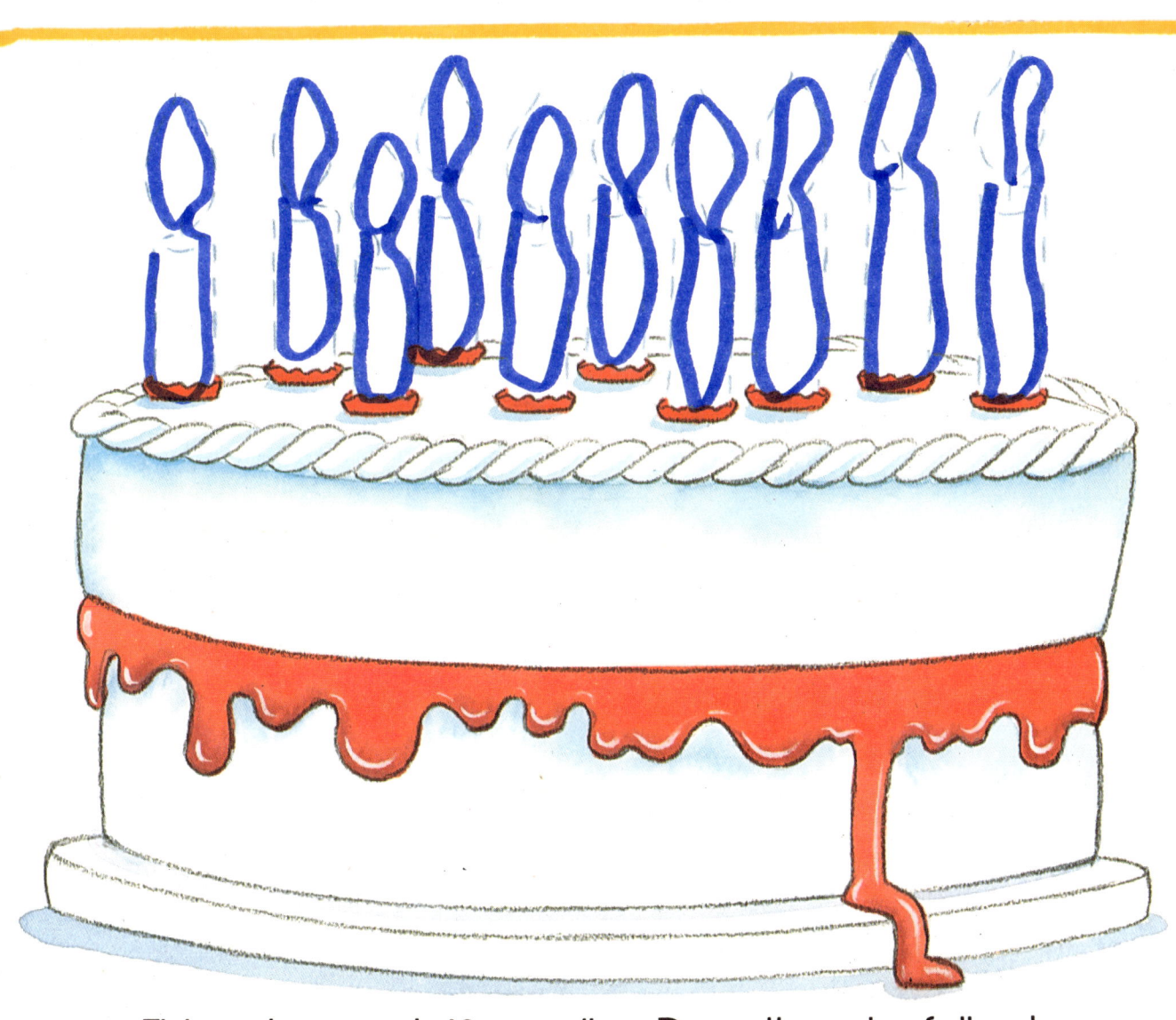

10 10 10 10 10 10 10 10

This cake needs 10 candles. Draw them by following the dotted lines.

eleven

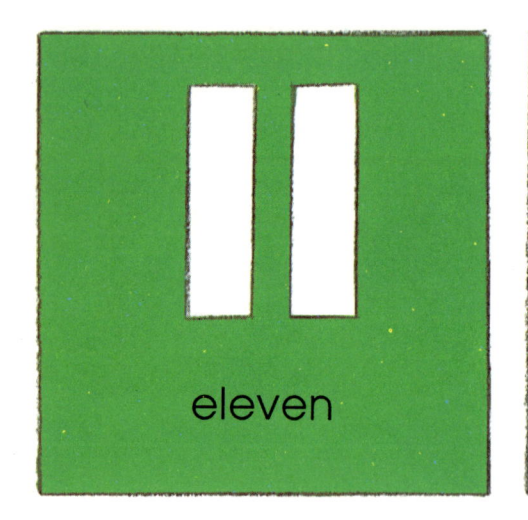

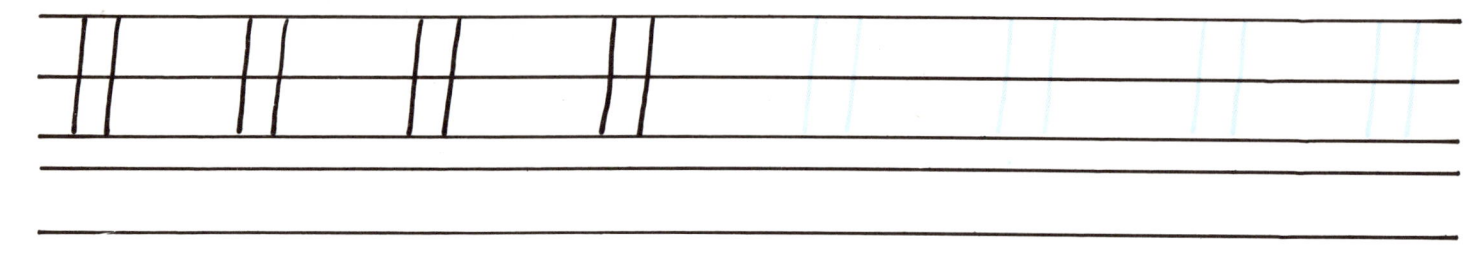

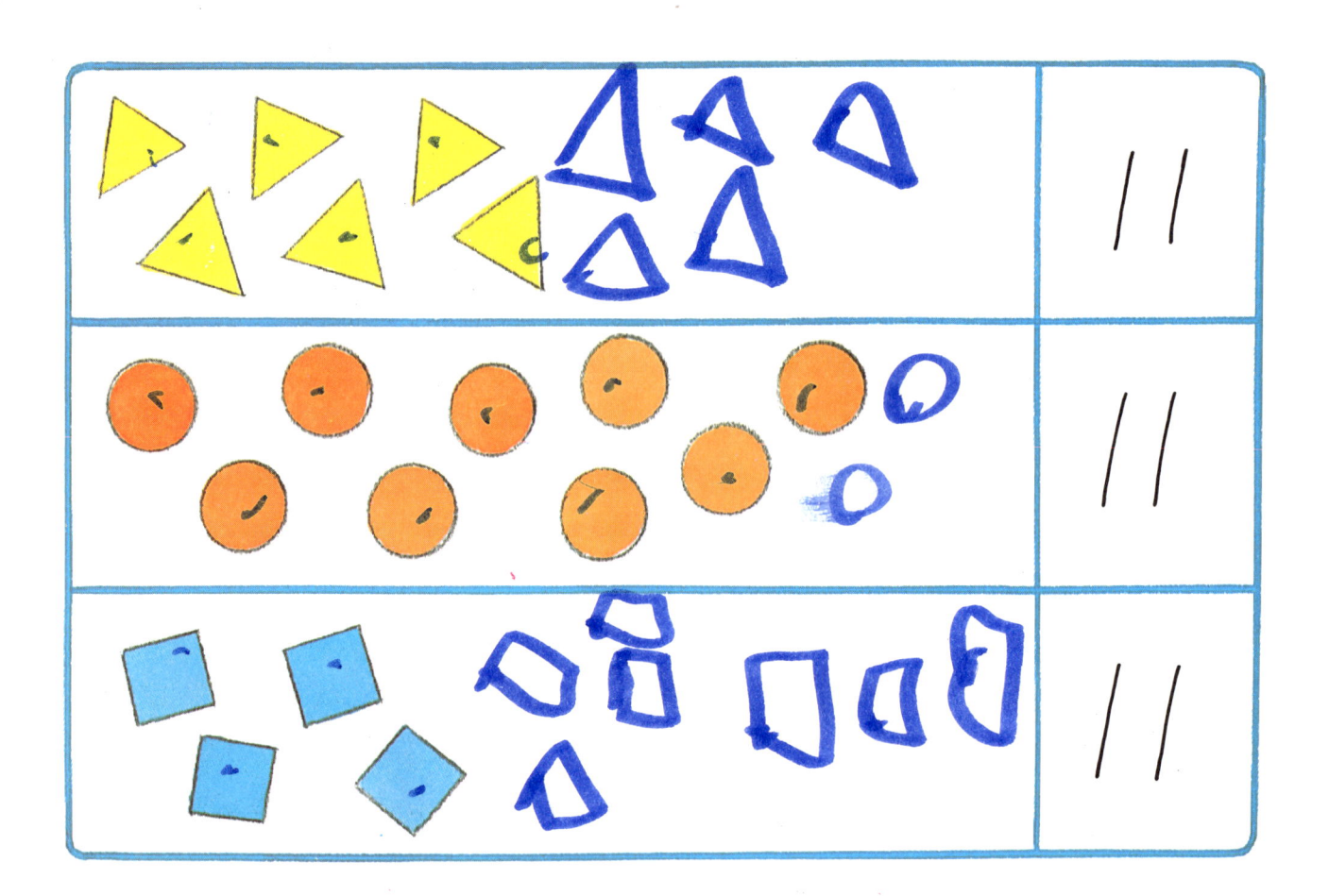

Count the shapes in each section and draw more shapes to make 11 in each. Now colour in the shapes you have drawn.

12

twelve

Trace over the other half of this leopard's face.
Draw in some spots so that he has 12 in all and colour him in.

13

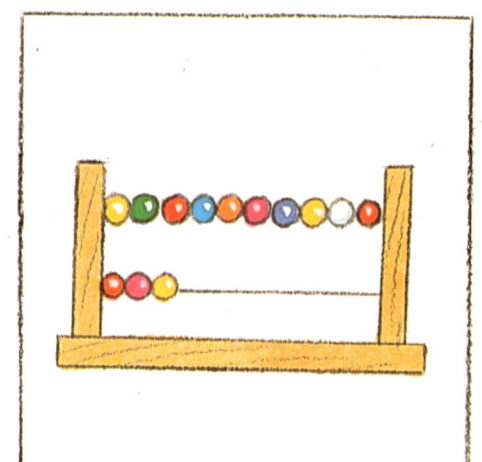

thirteen

13　13　13　13

Only one of these flowers has 13 petals. Find out which one it is and draw a circle round it.

14 fourteen

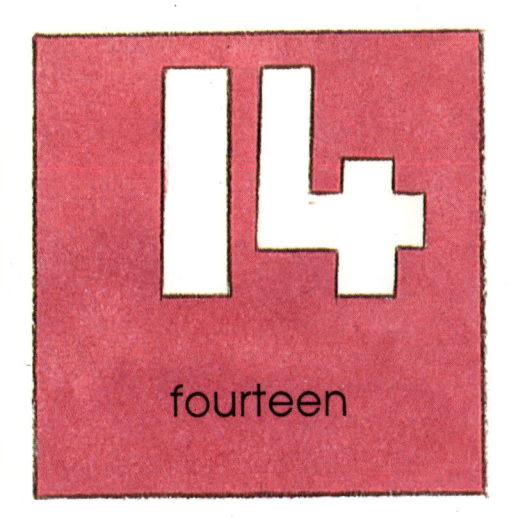

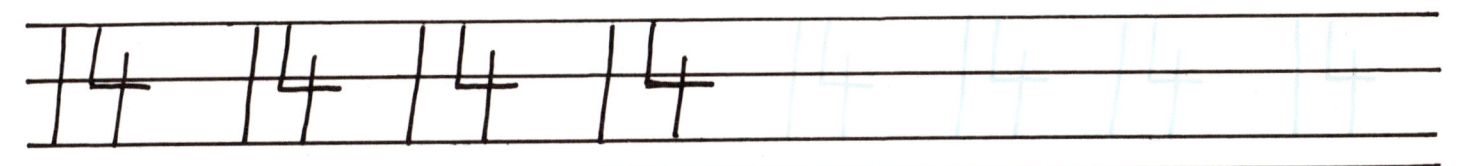

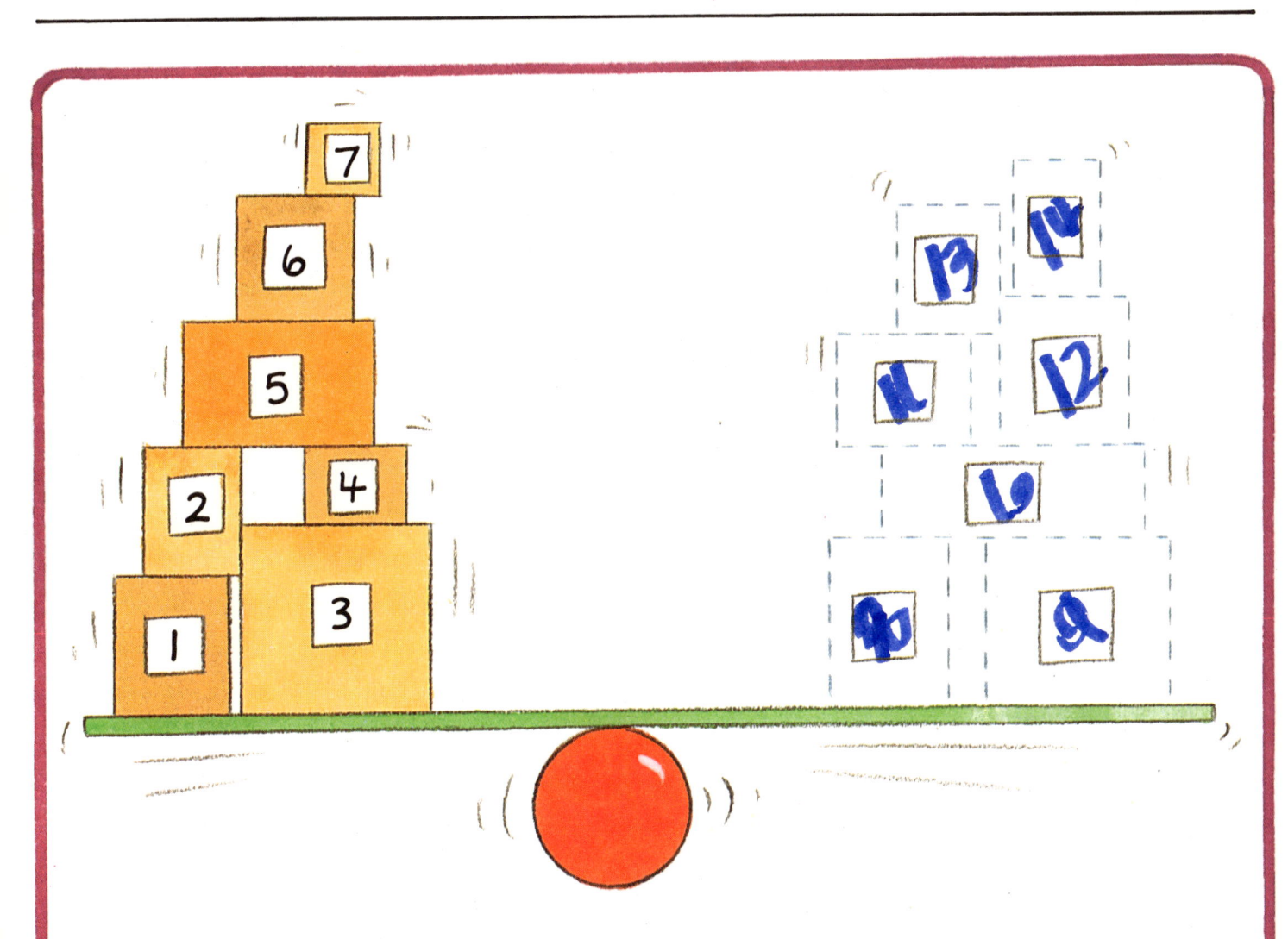

14 14 14 14 14 14 14

The see-saw needs balancing. Count the parcels on the left-hand side and draw in the same number on the right. Then number those parcels from 8 to 14.

15 fifteen

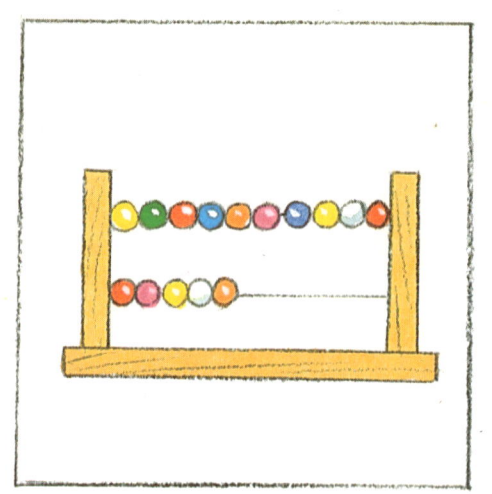

15 15 15 15

Join the dots by following the numbers from 1 to 15 and see who is sitting by the toys.

16
sixteen

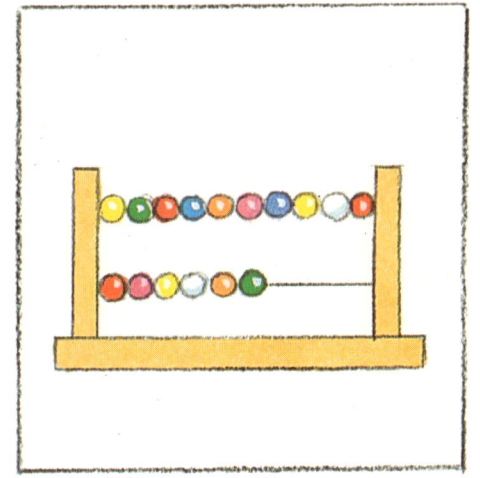

16 16 16 16 16 16 16

How many fingers does this space alien have? Count them and write the number on his nose.

17
seventeen

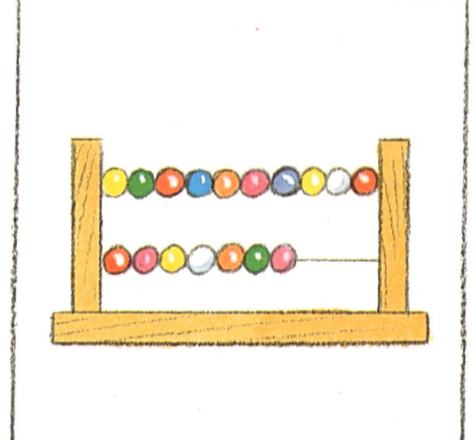

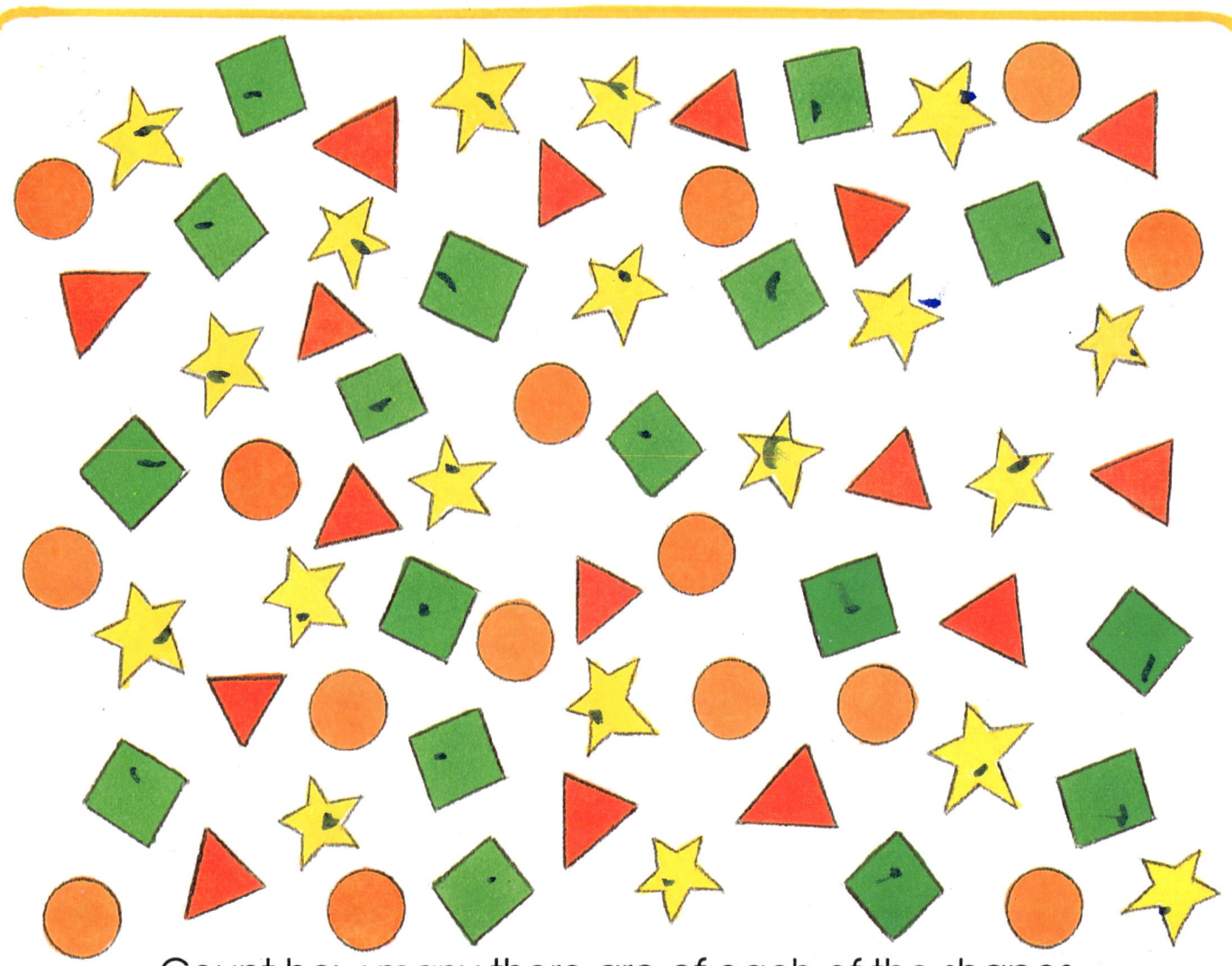

17 17 17 17

Count how many there are of each of the shapes above. There are 17 of one of them. Which one is it? Draw the shape in the box.

18
eighteen

18 18 18 18 18 18 18 18

Count the leaves on the branches above to find which branch has 18 leaves and draw a circle round that branch.

19 nineteen

19 19 19 19 19 19 19 19

How many carrots do you think the rabbit can eat? Fill in all the missing numbers to find out.

20 twenty

20 20 20 20 20 20 20 20

Count the objects in each group and then draw a line from the group to its correct number.

18
19
20

🌙	1
🧤	2
🎁	3
🖌	4
🍦	5
🎈	6
🧁	7
🚩	8
🥕	9
🔴	10

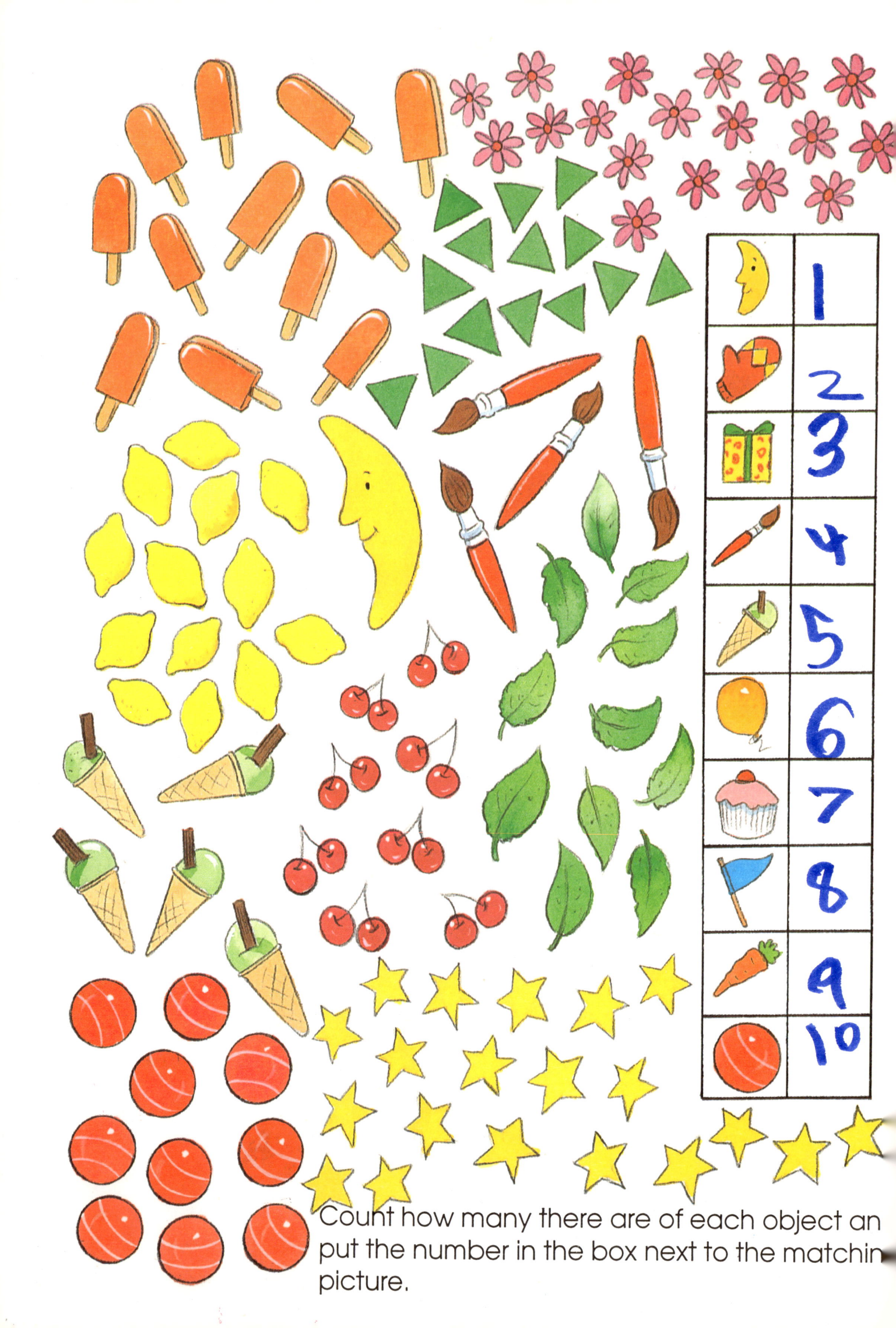

Count how many there are of each object and put the number in the box next to the matching picture.

🍃	11
🍦	12
🍋	13
△	14
🍊	15
🍒	16
🍏	17
🌸	18
✏️	19
⭐	20

Look at the picture below. How many creatures can you see? When you have counted them, first colour the one with 17 stripes, then the one with 8 diamonds, then the one with 20 circles, then the one with 14 triangles and finally the one with 10 spots. When you have done that colour the rest of the picture.

I can see .... creatures in this picture.

Now you will find that it is quite easy to count to 100.
Fill in the missing numbers that you have already learnt and use this table to help you to count to 100.

1	2	3		5	6	7	8		10
11		13	14	15		17	18	19	
21	22	23	24	25	26	27	28	29	30
31	32	33	34	35	36	37	38	39	40
41	42	43	44	45	46	47	48	49	50
51	52	53	54	55	56	57	58	59	60
61	62	63	64	65	66	67	68	69	70
71	72	73	74	75	76	77	78	79	80
81	82	83	84	85	86	87	88	89	90
91	92	93	94	95	96	97	98	99	100

Colour in all the numbers below and then write them in the correct order in the boxes: 1 to 10 in the left-hand column and 11 to 20 in the right-hand column.